D0393941

A

PRECIOUS MOMENTS™

GIFT OF LOVE

FOR YOU

Given to _____

On this _____ day of _____

By_____

With this special message . . .

_____

_____

_____

GIFT OF LOVE

Copyright © illustrations 1989 by Sam Butcher
Copyright © text 1989 by Sam Butcher and Carol C. Steele

All rights reserved. Written permission must be secured from
the publisher to use or reproduce any part of this book.

Published in Nashville, Tennessee, by Thomas Nelson, Inc.,
and distributed in Canada by Lawson Falle, Ltd., Cambridge,
Ontario.

Printed in the United States of America.
ISBN: 0-8407-7164-9

9 10 - 97 96

A

PRECIOUS MOMENTS™

GIFT OF LOVE

Illustrations by SAM BUTCHER
Poems by
SAM BUTCHER and CAROL C. STEELE

THOMAS NELSON PUBLISHERS
Nashville

THEE I LOVE

I love you, oh, so very much—
I've carved it on a tree!
I want to tell the whole wide world
How much you mean to me.

I think my trusty pocketknife
Has made my message plain.
And best of all it won't wash off
In case we have some rain.

My love will grow as years go by.
And when we're old and gray,
We can come and look again
At what I've carved today.

THE PERFECT RECIPE

God made the perfect recipe
When he made you, my love;
For all the right ingredients
Were sent from up above.

A dash of sweetness, pinch of fun,
A cup of love, then he was done.
He simply chose to bless me too
By giving me a friend like you.

LOVE COVERS ALL

Loving is sharing
And caring
And giving
Your heart in all that you do.

Loving is hoping
And coping
And spending
My very last penny on you.

Loving is healing—
Forgiving,
Forgetting—
The hurts of the present and past.

Loving is smiling
And laughing
And living
Each day as if it's your last.

LOVE ONE ANOTHER

There's nothing quite as wonderful
As loving one another.
In fact, the Lord has clearly said
That we should love our brother.

To share our love with someone else
Brings such a peace within.
And if we do, we'll always find
We're loved right back again.

I THANK THE LORD FOR YOU

Dear Friend, you are so special.
You are a gift of love,
And sent to fill my life with joy
From heaven up above.

You bring me so much happiness
By little things you do.
I thank the Lord for sending me
A friend as dear as you!

YOU HAVE TOUCHED SO MANY HEARTS

You have touched so many hearts
With all the love you've shown.
You have shared your inner strength
Through the seeds of love you've sown.

You seem to warm so many hearts
By just the way you smile,
And those who know you all agree
You go the extra mile.

We're so thankful to the Lord
Because we know it's true
That he could trust your willing heart
To do what he would do.

MY FAVORITE FRIEND

Whenever I think of my favorite friend,
My heart smiles once, then over again.

If one of us hurts, the other is there;
If one has no money, the other will share.

If one has a problem and can't find the way,
The other is there with something to say.

There's no doubt about it, I know I am blessed
To have found a sweet friend who is truly the best!

LOVE IS THE GLUE

He who has a loving heart
Can mend the things
That fall apart.

TO A VERY SPECIAL FRIEND

Gifts of kindness, caring too,
Come only from a friend like you.

Nothing you could ever do,
Will change the love I have for you.

HE CARES FOR YOU

Can we walk among the lilies
And still not be aware
As we behold their royal robes
That somehow, God is there?

Does he not feed the sparrow
And bathe the rose with dew?
If he then watches over these,
Think how much he cares for you!

I LOVE YOU, FRIEND

I'd like to take the time to say,
"I love you, Friend," in every way.

You mean so very much to me;
You're all I think a friend should be.

YOU ARE A TREASURE TO ME

That which means the most to me
Is priceless, yet it's also free,
Like stars that twinkle in the sky
And memories of days gone by.

But I have found that even this
Could never bring the happiness
I find in quiet moments when
I think of you, my precious friend.

TO TELL THE TOOTH
YOU'RE SPECIAL

I think you're something special
Because you are so sweet,
And just to be around you
Is always such a treat.

You never seem to get upset
And always have a way
Of giving me assurance that
Our friendship won't decay.

TO MY DEER FRIEND

Of all the creatures running free,
The one that means the most to me
Is the deer who gently runs
Beneath the warm and noonday sun.

To watch her in the morning dew,
Reminds me, oh, so much of you,
Because she has a special way
Of adding beauty to my day.

GOD LOVES A CHEERFUL GIVER

There's no sense in giving
If not from the heart,
For that is where loving
And giving both start.

There's no need for sharing
If it's not true
That your reason for sharing
Is because you want to.

If you're going to give
Then do it because
The gift comes from a heart
Overflowing with love.

A BOUQUET FROM HEAVEN

May each day unfold for you
Like roses, sparkling with dew,
That open to the morning sun
And bloom until the day is done.

And may each passing moment bring
A song as pure as angels sing
But may there be above all things
A peace that only God can bring.

FRIENDS NEVER DRIFT APART

Because you are my special friend
My life means so much more.
You've brought more joy and blessings
Than I've ever felt before.

I'll spend a lifetime telling you,
With help from God above,
Just how much you mean to me
And how precious is our love.

LET'S KEEP IN TOUCH

Let's keep in touch
Throughout the years
And let us not forget
The happy times
That we both shared
From the day we met.

LOVE

Seasons change, friends move away,
And life goes on from day to day.
Flowers fade and streams go dry
And many times we wonder why.

Yet we can always be assured,
Because God tells us in his Word,
That unlike changes in the weather
Love goes on and lasts forever.